CAREER
COUNSELLING
FOR EXECUTIVES

CAREER COUNSELLING
FOR EXECUTIVES

•

A GUIDE TO SELECTING
OUTPLACEMENT, REDEPLOYMENT
AND CAREER MANAGEMENT SERVICES

•

GODFREY GOLZEN

Published for

Coutts
Career Consultants Ltd

by
Kogan Page Ltd

First published in 1988
by Kogan Page Limited, 120 Pentonville Road, London N1 9JN
for Coutts Career Consultants Ltd

Typeset by DP Photosetting, Aylesbury, Bucks
Printed and bound in Great Britain by
Martins of Berwick, Ltd

British Library Cataloguing in Publication Data
Golzen, Godfrey
    Career counselling for executives.
    1. Managers. Careers. Development.
    I. Title
    658.4'09

ISBN 1-85091-686-1

FOREWORD

by Sir John Cuckney

Chairman of 3i Group plc, Royal Insurance plc, and Westland Group plc

At one time we could all expect to be with the firm we joined from school or college for the rest of our working lives.

Now, for a variety of reasons, people are learning daily that those times are past, and that job mobility is with us to stay.

Forced departure from a job – through redundancy, for example – is traumatic. It is traumatic to the people who must leave, and indeed to those who remain. I know from my own experience in industry that the health of the firm (and the security of work for those who remain) sometimes requires the very painful decision of enforced redundancy.

The company's responsibility is primarily to those who remain, yet it would be quite wrong to abandon those who must go.

The virtues of external consultancies, experienced in assisting people through this period, become apparent. They offer, to company and individual, the objectivity and specialised assistance required to get back on the road to productivity.

Choosing such a consultancy is made easier when you know what to look for. I welcome this book, published by the UK's leading consultancy and written by a respected authority on the subject, because it states clearly what standards of professionalism and service should be demanded.

I recommend the book to all managers, people involved in personnel decisions, and – indeed – anyone considering a career change.

Sir John Cuckney

CONTENTS

Foreword   5

1 The Objectives of this Study   9

2 The Background of Change   11

3 Who is at Risk?   15

4 The Role of Career Counselling   19

5 First Steps in Career Counselling   27

6 How Career Counselling Proceeds   33

7 What Career Counselling Can - and Cannot - Deliver   41

8 The Issue of Fees   47

9 Towards a Code of Practice   51

"

A view of what career
counselling is, what
directions it is taking
and what good practice ought to be

"

THE OBJECTIVES OF THIS STUDY

1

Growth industry

The number of firms involved in career counselling and outplacement in the UK is growing. The new edition of *Redundancy Counselling For Managers* (IPM) lists 19, with still more being established. Variations in practice, orientation of counselling and, to be frank, reputation, are beginning to develop. It would be desirable, perhaps, if they could get together to create a code of practice, as in the USA. There, no less than 154 firms are involved in career consultancy, and growth is at a rate of 35% per annum.

Making the right choice

Coutts Career Consultants (hereafter referred to as Coutts) have commissioned this book to offer a view of what career counselling is, what directions it is taking and what good practice ought to be. It is their hope that this book will be useful to those who are not fully familiar with the concept and who may want to make a choice between the options on offer, either for themselves or for employees who have to make a change in the direction of their career.

> **"**
> Executive mobility,
> forced or otherwise,
> is not a temporary phenomenon
> **"**

THE BACKGROUND OF CHANGE

2

Making the tough decisions

Most managers today not only have to make career choices for themselves but, increasingly, have to make tough decisions that affect the careers of others, both executive and other staff. Statistics about executive job mobility are hard to find or verify. A probable figure can be inferred from the circulation figures of the Manpower Services Commission's *Executive Post*. With a controlled circulation of 120,000 made up of professionals and executives on the move, this represents 4·5% of the current total of unemployed in the country.

Executive mobility, forced or otherwise, is not a temporary phenomenon. Recruitment pages are crammed with advertising and there is a boom in the demand for executive search. These trends are simply further aspects of change which, as much as 'excellence', is the management slogan of the decade. Change as a condition of corporate survival is one of a number of factors which have come together to ensure that careers are very much less stable than they were even a decade ago.

The importance of 'change' in the corporate world

- The spread of information technology has increasingly begun to automate decision-making at intermediate levels in organisations. Activities, such as design, that used to call for a fair amount of judgement, are becoming dominated by computers.

- Decision-making has moved up the organisation, growing in scale but being made by fewer managers.

- There is less room at the top, trapping more managers in the middle of organisatons. At the same time, these middle sectors are being squeezed by the need to control costs in order to remain competitive. Jobs that do not have a function which can show above-the-line benefits are rigorously evaluated. Yesterday's sidings for those who could not get to the top are disappearing.

- Even functions with long-term benefits, like R&D, can come under threat from shareholders or directors who want immediately demonstrable results.

- Mergers and acquisitions have reached unprecedented heights. Consequent 'rationalisations' of jobs and functions are as likely to hit white-collar as blue-collar employees. 27% of the directors of target companies in a merger leave within the first year, with a similar pattern likely among other senior managers.* The main reason is difficulty in adapting to the new corporate culture.

● In the public sector, these trends have meant a growing number of organisations abandoning what have, up to now, been virtual guarantees of lifetime careers. Even in Japan, where lifetime one-company careers have always been part of the culture, increased job mobility is now apparent.

* *Acquisitions: the human factor.* J W Hunt, and others (pub: Egon Zehnder and the London Business School)

""

Post war babies, and the
middle-ranked and middle-aged
are particularly at risk

""

WHO
IS AT RISK?

3

The 'baby boomers'

Certain age groups are particularly at risk. There are those born in the immediate post war years. They are now in their crucial mid-career period of 37-43. To be winners, they face an unusually high number of competitors. Even the high flyers are continually being re-assessed.

For whatever reason – from promotion beyond their level of competence, to lack of interpersonal skills – the losers are singled out, and the barriers are brought down on them. Their problems are heightened because their financial and family commitments are often at their peak at this time of life.

The middle-ranked and middle-aged

The other endangered demographic group are those between 45-55, who occupy the middle and upper middle ranks in organisations. Members of this group may find that the technological changes have outstripped them. They discover computer literacy is now a bigger gap between the generations than age.

They may also find it more difficult to adapt to new ways of working, particularly if they have spent a long

Early retirement not feasible

time in the same organisation. For those at the younger end of this age span, early retirement is usually neither a financially nor a psychologically feasible option.

A feature of the 45-55 year age group is the individual's questioning of his or her life direction and of relationships at work and at home.

The plus side

On the plus side, this age group may be more willing to risk trying new things; and may be less weighed by external or family commitments than younger colleagues.

"

Outplacement assists the
clean break that is best
for both the individual
and the organisation

"

THE
ROLE OF CAREER
COUNSELLING

4

Defining the terms

The terms 'career counselling' and 'outplacement' are broadly interchangeable. However, in practice 'outplacement' is used to describe the sponsorship of a client by a firm as part of a severance package.

The individual is always termed the 'client', with the firm or organisation called the 'sponsor'.

The language emphasises that the career consultancy is working to the individual's needs, although paid by a sponsoring organisation.

How long between jobs?

The Department of Trade and Industry's *Employment Gazette** shows that 60% of those out of work between the ages of 25 and 54 take over 26 weeks to find a new job. Indeed, 48% are still unemployed after a full year.

Reducing the time

There is, however, widespread evidence that in the same age groups those who have gone through career counselling

* Source: Dept of Trade & Industry *Employment Gazette*, November 1987

or outplacement are able to reduce this time significantly.

Coutts, one of the UK's longest established firms in career consultancy and outplacement, claim an average 15 weeks before re-employment of what they term a 'standard candidate' – someone aged between 35 and 40, earning between £20,000 and £30,000 a year.

Factors which may delay success

A number of factors which can influence the period of time spent between positions may be identified. Stephen Johnson, managing director of Coutts, notes as 'difficult' cases candidates who are over 55 and what he terms 'stickers', 'bouncers' and 'changers':

- *Stickers*: Executives who have remained a long time in one job or within the same organisation without any variety of executive experience. Therefore, the task of marketing their skills and presenting themselves at interviews has become an unfamiliar one to them. They may also feel diffident about 'selling themselves'.

- *Bouncers*: those whose tenure in their last job was unusually short. This fact obviously bothers potential employers and affects the applicant's confidence.

- *Changers*: people whose CVs show frequent job changes and relatively short periods of tenure. That again raises question marks about the person's stability and commitment.

The trauma of redundancy

Whatever the circumstances, though, executives who find their career with an organisation terminated or under threat will face, sooner or later, some kind of psychological trauma. 'Suddenly, from having the security, the status, the physical comforts of a company car and other facilities, he becomes a man adrift,' says an article in *The Director*.*

(The same fate can, of course, overtake women!) 'His world is shattered and, often worse, he has to break the news to a wife and family who may become frightened at the possibilities of unemployment.'

Helping those affected to get over the shock – crisis counselling – is the first step in the services offered by career counselling.

The next step is to establish the future career direction for the person in the light of his or her interests, ambitions and aptitudes. This is followed by general search advice: opening out the search into the unadvertised job market and researching companies that have been identified as prospects.

Coaching in the techniques of CV writing, and handling interviews and job offers, may also be given.

* Facing the Future: Career Counselling, *The Director*, October 1984.

Identifying the skills

The sequence is important, because the shock of job loss can often seem to outweigh – in his or her own mind – the marketable skills which every client has. Such a negative psychological attitude has to be altered before the job search can take a coherent shape – or even proceed at all.

Indeed, it may be that skills identified in the course of a detailed Career Survey (which may precede the job-hunting process itself) suit the person for a slot elsewhere in their current organisation.

The options

More often, though, the options to be considered are:

- Moving to another organisation in the same sector
- Moving to a job in another sector altogether
- Self-employment
- Early retirement

Career counselling can be, and often is, part of the job-finding strategy for individual executives at senior levels – those who have been earning £20,000 a year or more.

Extending the personnel function

There is now a growing recognition by employers that outplacement is an important extension of their own personnel function when it comes to handling the difficult problems associated with redundancy at every level.

A full outplacement/career counselling programme lasts until the client finds another job and even for the first months in a new assignment. The full range of expertise to provide this kind of professional help in-depth and over an indefinite period of time is seldom available in-house.

Providing the clean break between employer and employee

In fact, it is not desirable that it should be. Both for psychological and practical reasons, it is best that it should be provided by a third party not directly associated with the employer, and not burdened with any of the emotions that the circumstances of severance may have aroused.

Outplacement, preferably made available right away as part of the severance package, assists the clean break that is best both for the individual and the organisation.

Benefits for the employer

Enlightened self-interest also plays a part in outplacement. Companies need to be seen to be behaving in a caring way to employees, at whatever level, who have fallen victim, for whatever reason, to the need for change. That is a matter of internal morale and external reputation, which affects recruitment and the position of the organisation in the community.

An employer is not obliged to pay a parting executive a large sum of money. However, it is in the employer's own interest to do what he reasonably can to get that executive back to work as quickly as possible with the least personal damage. Experienced career consultants state that over-generous payments can actually make early resettlement more difficult. Large payments tempt the newly redundant to delay rather than focus on their new 'full-time' job: the job search itself.

For *all* employee levels

The usefulness of counselling is not restricted to middle or senior management. A growing trend is for employers to offer it in the form of group training and individual counselling to those below management level when large-scale redundancies take place – for instance, in the case of plant closures.

"

The aim (first step) is
to identify the right track
on which the job search
should proceed in the light
of career history to date

"

FIRST STEPS IN CAREER COUNSELLING

5

Career counselling developed in modern terms in the 1960s when redundancy first began to affect executives. At that stage, UK practitioners were influenced by American models where the concept of 'counselling' had been most strongly developed. The process was much concerned with clinically oriented psychological testing, followed by therapy-led counselling sessions.

While that view of career counselling and outplacement still persists in the minds of some people, the fact is that a sturdy British version has since developed. The new version is very much related to the practicalities of the job market. Indeed, a similar trend has now been noted in career counselling in the USA.

In the UK, Coutts are easily the longest established firm in the field. They began in 1908 and an important part of their business was in helping returning expatriates to find jobs in the UK. They were also leaders in developing sponsored outplacement in the 1970s.

The main strands in consultancy process

A report produced by the *Economist Intelligence Unit* identifies four main strands in the process.

- **Crisis counselling** deals with the immediate aftermath of a redundancy announcement – how to handle the shock, what to tell one's family and friends.

- **Career counselling** is concerned with establishing the future direction of a career in the light of ambitions, interests and aptitudes.

- **Coaching** involves practical help with CV writing, answering job advertisements, interview techniques and methods of handling job offers, networking and use of contacts.

- **Advice in the job search** ranges from opening up the search from the advertised to the unadvertised job market, to providing objective information and research on companies to whom applications or 'on spec' letters are being addressed.

Allocating time

The percentage of total search time to be spent on each of these phases varies with the individual.

Stephen Johnson, managing director of Coutts, comments: 'There are some people who need a lot of crisis counselling before you can launch them on the market. At the other extreme, you might find someone who knows what he wants to do and is well qualified to do it, but his presentation is poor. In that case we'd want to put our emphasis on coaching.'

Taking the first step

The first step is an informal, free, preliminary chat with the client. In some cases this results in a decision not to proceed further. The client may feel that the services being offered are not what he or she wants. Alternatively, the counselling firm may feel that it cannot help the client. Some critics have felt that, by possibly eliminating potentially difficult cases, consultants are able to preserve the almost 100% success rates which their clients achieve.

Career counsellors deny this. A full counselling course typically costs around 15% of last salary and they say it would be invidious to take money from people whom they cannot be reasonably sure of helping.

When not to proceed with counselling

Characteristically, counselling is not proceeded with when a client has clearly been sent for outplacement by a sponsor company against his or her will and maintains that attitude; when expectations of what counselling can achieve are incorrigibly unrealistic; when a client's state of mind is such that he or she clearly needs other forms of specialist counselling before career counselling can be of benefit. Cases in point would be alcoholism or severe behavioural disturbances.

The first step: Career Survey

The next step, for those who wish to proceed, is to allocate to the client a consultant who will be in charge of his or her case. The consultant will begin by conducting a detailed Career Survey.

While the practice differs between firms, the objective is the same. Some firms ask clients to write an extensive, detailed, career-based autobiography, focusing on achievements, personal characteristics, values, interests and aims.

Psychometric testing

Coutts, for instance, use psychometric testing of aptitudes and personality by an in-house occupational psychologist, as well as extensive interviewing and assessment by the consultant in charge. The client would also have to undertake some degree of self-assessment. The process takes about ten hours.

The aim is to identify the right track on which the job search should proceed in the light of career history to date, career aims, and possible constraints which may be determined by aptitudes, qualifications, needs and personal circumstances.

Crisis counselling

The consultant also has to determine the degree of crisis counselling that may be required. Like many other facets of career counselling, this is not something to be confined to a particular phase of the search. It often happens that a client begins by feeling very confident, but that confidence is eroded when setbacks occur – as they almost always do at some stage.

However, this does depend on the individual and the circumstances. In some cases, the most urgent need for crisis counselling can come immediately after severance. It is sometimes advisable, in outplacement, to have a career consultant on hand following the termination interviews.

24 hour support

Support and encouragement from the consultant is then very helpful and a number of consultancy firms make it a rule that their consultants should be available and accessible out of hours to their particular clients.

Should the spouse be involved?

Another area where practice may differ between consultancy firms is the extent to which spouses are involved. Some firms insist that spouse or partner should be part of the process as well, because of the need for family understanding and support during the search. Coutts and several others take the view that whether spouse/partners should be brought in should depend on what the personality tests and interviews reveal about the client. The client, too, should agree on the action.

"

In career terms, the past
is only useful for the lessons
it carries for the future

"

HOW CAREER COUNSELLING PROCEEDS

6

Setting the objective

The primary objective of the counselling process is to assist the client to a job finding success. The career analysis, which should be continually refined, is the key element in this. From it, the client and the consultant select the right mix of career advice, coaching and job finding back-up that will eventually lead to success.

Consultants should never allow clients to dwell on past grievances, however real these may be. In career terms the past is only useful for the lessons it carries for the future, and in the compilation of the CV.

The CV

The CV should be a positive job-getting tool, which quantifies achievements and sets out career objectives. Too often it reads like a career obituary, or at best a 'laundry list' of previous appointments.

There are a number of schools of thought among career consultants about how to assist clients in preparing their CVs. Some produce CVs from data produced by clients, rather in the manner of firms offering CV writing services. Others, such as Coutts, coach clients in CV writing. The resulting documents should be professionally edited by someone in the consulting firm, but should remain in essence the client's own effort.

A sound reason for clients writing their own CVs is that such an exercise often shows up weaknesses in communication skills. Clients also benefit from being trained in the principles of CV writing, because slightly different CVs will have to be produced for various applications. (Some recruiters are put off by 'manufactured' CVs. Conversely job-relevant ones are always taken seriously.)

Support services

All good career consultancies provide secretarial services for producing professionally typed and well laid-out CVs and letters of application. Some charge an additional fee for this service.

Other services may also be charged. At least one outplacement firm, for instance, allows its clients to telephone from their office without restriction, but they add a sum for expenses to their fee for such purposes.

There are also varying practices on whether or not financial and legal advice is included as part of the service, or whether the consultancy confines its role to recommending reliable professionals in these spheres.

Facility services

How much facility back-up should generally be given? Here again there are differing views. Some very good firms provide workspaces and encourage clients to conduct much of their search from them on the grounds that it is beneficial to simulate a working environment as far as possible.

Other equally good consultancies feel that too much contact with fellow clients tends to produce a 'talking shop' atmosphere – and long pub lunches! It can lead to clients focusing on their present unemployment rather than on their future.

Developing contacts

Again, it depends on the individual whether contact with others in the same situation is used constructively or not.

However, informal exchanges of views between fellow clients can certainly be constructive as part of 'contact development', which all career consultants regard as crucial to the job search at any level.

Right at the beginning of the process, clients are asked to list all the people they know who might be worth talking to about job prospects. The list should extend beyond those who are in a position to make hiring decisions, to include people with a knowledge of the job search target areas or those who have access to such individuals.

Clients are encouraged to contact these people to gain information about the target search area, and any news which may indicate unadvertised vacancies (about 60% of jobs filled come into this category). They may also obtain further contact names. It is not the purpose of a contact interview to gain a job. Indeed, clients are actively discouraged from soliciting offers during such interviews.

The contact meetings help to restore the client's 'currency', ie up-to-date knowledge of that business sector.

He must know what is going on in the market he wants to enter, not just what he did in his last job.

The contact development technique does sometimes result in a job offer being made when the right person walks through the door at the right time, but the main object is to practise and gain confidence in the techniques of being interviewed.

Learning sessions

The consultant will help the client to identify problem questions, and develop true and convincing answers.

The consultancy should be able to reinforce these vital techniques, firstly by recording dummy interviews on video, so that clients can have the sometimes salutary experience of seeing themselves as others see them, and secondly by extensive de-briefing sessions with their clients after each interview.

Pre-interview briefing, both for contact development and 'the real thing' is equally important, and here the consultancy's research facilities are vitally important.

Research facilities

These can vary widely in sophistication. Coutts, for instance, employ a qualified librarian full time as research manager. He is able to provide clients with anything from brochures, reports, relevant trade magazines, Extel cards and newspaper clippings on target companies to hard copy extracted from databases about current projects and contracts.

At the other end of the scale are the consultancies whose facilities do not go much beyond providing shelves of such standard references as *Who's Who*, the *Kompass Register, Key British Enterprises** and so forth.

Negotiating an offer

Career consultancy also fulfils an important role when an offer has actually been made. A good consultant should satisfy himself that the offer is the right one for the client in relation to what is now known about that person.

Both consultant and client should be aware that getting the client 'off the books' at the first opportunity may

---

* All usually available in a public library

mean that past career mistakes are simply repeated elsewhere.

Clients often need some coaching on how to handle a job offer. At what point, for instance, should salary and benefits be discussed? How much room is there to negotiate better terms?

Experienced consultancies agree – clients are not good at getting the best deal for themselves and often err on the side of either timidity or over-assertiveness.

A consultant with experience of a variety of negotiating positions, and sometimes of the culture of the actual firm involved, can often give invaluable advice to his client at this point.

Self-employment

Some clients may decide that they want to set up in business for themselves. In the case of people over 55, those with hard to market skills or those who show a pattern of being uncomfortable in subordinate positions, self-employment is potentially the best option.

Here again, consultants should be able to give a frank assessment on a client's aptitude for self-employment that may be at least partly based on the results of psychometric testing, but resources and business experience are also important. Ideally, the consultant should take the client as far as the formulation of a business plan with which to approach funding sources. In areas of self-employment which require very little capital, such as freelance consultancy, very similar principles still apply.

"

The emphasis is on showing
the client how to do it,
rather than doing it for them

"

WHAT CAREER COUNSELLING CAN – AND CANNOT – DELIVER

7

***Not* a job finding agency**

The most common misapprehension about career consultancies/ outplacement firms is that they 'find jobs' for clients. This is emphatically not so and it would in fact be a breach of the Employment Agencies Act to take money from people for that purpose.

The Institute of Personnel Management states very broadly what career counselling does by saying that it 'helps the client to evaluate different possibilities and decide which, if any, to pursue'.

**Gaining interviews
Generating offers**

After the initial assessment by the client and the consultant, a two-tier process begins. Coutts describes this as 'marketing to generate interviews', and once the interviews have been arranged, 'sales to generate offers'.

Career consultancies do promote their clients to such recruitment intermediaries as headhunters by selectively sending them CVs of suitable people and by maintaining ongoing lines of communication with job market insiders. However, the emphasis is on showing the clients how to do it, rather than doing it for them.

The general opinion is that for a consultancy to arrange interviews for its clients is rather like the kind of arranged marriage where the groom does not see the bride until the ceremony. On the other hand, there may on occasion be valid reasons for this – for instance, if the client is a working expatriate.

Reducing the waiting time

The period of time between jobs varies according to age and marketability of experience and qualifications, but waiting is almost always involved.

It is some consolation that the use of an outplacement agency significantly reduces the average waiting time.*

Coping with waiting

Bearing in mind that statistics show that even independent job seekers are likely to be placed inside a year, the strains of waiting may be more psychological than financial (at least initially).

Outplaced clients who have been sent by their employers will almost invariably have received a lump sum in compensation for loss of office; more

* See page 19

rarely they will still be on the employer's payroll until they find something else.

Even private clients are generally at a level where quite substantial amounts of compensation have been paid – up to a year's salary or occasionally more.

'Interim' employment

However, should clients find some form of interim paid employment and, if so, can career counselling firms be of any assistance in this sphere?

The general opinion is that the job search should be a full-time occupation. Nevertheless, where this is not possible, consultancies and outplacement firms do have contacts among headhunters and other recruitment intermediaries – and in industry in general – which could lead to short-term consultancies for clients.

There is a growing interest now in what is called 'interim management' – longer term temporary executive assignments. Well-respected outplacement firms are potential sources in the search for interim managers, but it has to be a matter of judgement whether a client should be recommended to pursue or take up offers of this kind.

The object is to find full-time employment, though a series of lucrative interim management posts can be a very acceptable alternative, especially for older clients.

Selecting the right programme

To some extent, what career consultancies can deliver depends on

43

what the client pays for. The full course may cost about 15% of last salary. There are, however, alternative courses to suit differing needs. Group

Group counselling

counselling for supervisory and shop floor staff, for instance, is based on seminars as well as individual contact related to a greatly intensified 'job shop' approach. In these instances, fees are charged on a per capita basis.

Individual executive counselling

Costing the programme

Individual executive counselling can also be menu-based: the initial Career Survey is followed by recommendations as to the areas where the client most needs coaching. An estimate of costs should also be given. Subsequent sessions can then be charged out on an hourly fee, as in any other kind of professional consultation, or paid for on a job cost basis.

Career self-management

As the notion of career self-management takes hold, individuals may well opt for this approach at critical points in their careers where they feel they might benefit from objective, qualified advice.

Selecting the consultancy

There are, of course, also qualitative differences between consultancies.

Local or national?

Some consulting firms have a number of branches throughout the country, giving them access to local markets and inside knowledge of them. Others are simply based in one location only.

Which to choose is a matter of individual judgement and may depend on the client's individual circumstances, such as the readiness or willingness to relocate. Generally, one should seek career advice in the area in which one wishes to work.

Selecting the consultant

Consultants vary too. As in every human activity, some are better than others; or the personal chemistry between client and consultant may not work.

It is important that clients should meet the consultant they will be dealing with before committing themselves to a particular choice.

Even then, they should be given the opportunity to switch, if the relationship does not develop smoothly.

> "
> Shortening the job search
> will lessen loss of earnings.
> This reduced loss is frequently
> greater than the consultant's fee
> "

THE
ISSUE OF FEES

8

How much?

The full career counselling/ outplacement service at executive level costs around 15% of the client's last salary. There are some variations within this.

Agreeing the fee

Some consulting firms put an upper limit on the lump sum, others take into account the value of the total remuneration package (which may be much larger than the salary element on its own) in calculating their fees. Some charge expenses on top of the percentage figure, others do not. There may also be differences in the way payment is made. Individuals, paying for counselling out of their own pocket, may be allowed to make staged payments.

Value for money

But whichever way these charges are made, career counselling is not cheap and it is sometimes criticised on those grounds. Critics, however, tend to overlook the key factors.

- The full counselling process is not complete until the client has found another job – the right job for the person concerned, not just any job. In some cases counselling even continues into the job induction period. In terms of time spent by consultants over the average four months of job hunting (and it does on occasion take longer with a difficult case) the fees compare favourably with the charges of other professional bodies.

- Set against earnings over a 20-year career span, the charges are in fact very reasonable. For instance, a person earning £25,000 a year would gross £500,000 over that period, without adjustments for inflation or higher earnings. Career counselling on that salary base would cost £3,750, less than two months' initial salary.

- Even in the immediate term, shortening the job search by six months would lessen loss of earnings by an appreciable amount, no matter what the salary level.

The fee level is often considerably less than those charged by headhunters, who may ask up to 33% of salary.

For the individual

Some private individuals may have considerable difficulty in paying a lump sum. They may not have been treated generously by their last employer (who may not have been in a position to do so), or have simply resigned without making any provision for severance.

There are also those who feel they only require guidance on specific areas of weakness, such as interview technique.

Then, it may be possible to negotiate a rate based on hourly charges. That would, however, not be open-ended until the client finds a job, as is the case with a full counselling programme.

Some consulting firms are introducing an hourly charge for individuals applying career self-management. Rather than looking to the employer to provide satisfactory career progression, individual executives are increasingly looking to career counselling as a professional service for advice, in much the same way as they might consult a solicitor, accountant or pension adviser.

"

The interest of the
individual client should be
paramount, regardless of
who is paying the fee

"

TOWARDS A CODE OF PRACTICE

9

We have already spelled out what clients and sponsoring firms could reasonably expect for their money. But career counselling/outplacement is now a fast growing £20 million a year business. And, as in any expanding market, a number of grey areas have developed.

Establishing good practice

Therefore, it might be helpful to those thinking of using counselling or of sponsoring outplacement to have some guidelines on conduct to be expected from a career consultancy.

The following guidelines, though not specifically demanded by legislation, are generally regarded in the career consultancy profession as good practice.

Such guidelines would also be a useful point of reference for those who are thinking of offering consultancy services.

Accepting assignments

• Consultancy firms should not accept assignments which they have reason to believe are unlikely to be successful due to factors outside their control – for instance, where the client has evident medical/psychiatric problems which require appropriate treatment before career counselling can serve any purpose.

Client's interest is paramount

- The interest of the individual client should be paramount. This applies regardless of who is paying the fee (company or the individual). However, it is not the role of career counselling to enter into grievances on behalf of the client.

Total confidentiality

- Any dealings between client and consultancy should be strictly confidential, no matter whether their content is personal or commercial. The sponsoring organisation should not see its employee's file.

Written terms of agreement

- In every case, the counselling process should be preceded by a written agreement between the client - or, in the case of outplacement, the sponsors - and the consultancy. This should specify exactly what services and other facilities or forms of material and psychological support are being offered for the agreed fee. Anything not listed should be understood to be excluded or subject to an extra charge.

Agreeing the fee

- If staged payments are to be made, the agreement should state when these are due. It should also indicate in which circumstances, if any, it can be terminated by either party; and in what circumstances, if any, refunds would be due to the client/sponsor in respect of payments already made.

Where there are options regarding the manner and amount of payment – for instance, where clients may be given the choice between taking the full counselling or outplacement programme or a shorter, less expensive version – such options should be made clear to them and their implications explained before they undertake any financial obligation.

A warranty period

• The agreement should say whether it includes a 'warranty period'; ie if the client finds a job and is again severed from it through no obvious fault of his or her own, such a warranty clause would allow further counselling without charge until the client is again placed. It would, however, set a time over which it is operative, rather like the warranty on some consumer durables.

Choosing the consultant

• The individuals being counselled should be given the opportunity of meeting the consultant who will be handling their case, prior to any commitment being made. If, during the course of counselling, clients wish to change consultant, they should be free to do so.

On the other hand, counselling firms should make every endeavour to keep the same consultant assigned to a client during the search period. They should not knowingly assign a consultant who has announced an intention of leaving the consultancy.

Determining the consultant's expertise

- Details of the consultant's own professional business background should be disclosed, when required. Although a 'trade fit' is not necessary between the consultant's experience and qualifications and the area of job search, consultants should have had experience at a level appropriate to their clients' circumstances.

Professional staff, such as occupational psychologists, should have recognised professional qualifications. They should also have received at least six weeks of training in counselling.

A consultancy should have an ongoing programme of continued professional development for its consultants, to keep up to date their understanding of developments in the corporate world and trends in the employment scene generally.

The consultant's caseload

- The caseload of the consultant attached to a particular assignment should be disclosed if required by the client or sponsor.

Practice varies between firms and an outplacement sponsor or a private client seeking counselling will have to make a personal judgement about whether the caseload of the counsellor is satisfactory for their needs.

The crucial period, when most attention is required, is in the earlier stages of the process. The client's needs also determine the degree of personal attention required from the counsellor: clients who have marked career difficulties will obviously need more time spent with them than those who have none.

Back-up support

● The level of back-up support services from non-counselling staff should also be assessed. As the job search gets under way, the need for the counsellor may lessen while the need for research staff and facilities, and other services such as self-help instructional manuals, will increase.

Validating the consultant's claims

● The counselling/outplacement firm should be able to substantiate any claims it makes about the level at which clients are finding jobs, and the length of time they are on the market.

Because of the confidentiality of career counselling and the reluctance of past clients to act as referees, it is often difficult to find individuals who will vouch for its effectiveness in their case.

However, consultants should certainly be able to validate what they say about what sponsors they have acted for and the extent and value of their contacts.

The key criteria for prospective clients and/or sponsors are the currency of both contacts and other sponsors. It is important to discover whether the named sponsors are continuing business relationships or whether it is a 'one-off' that may not have come to a satisfactory conclusion.

Career consultants only

● Some consultants are also directly or indirectly involved with recruitment and executive search. In the opinion of Coutts and other experienced firms, this is not a desirable practice. Firstly, they argue it puts such a firm in the position of competing with those to whom it should refer its clients.

Secondly, it arouses in other recruitment intermediaries the suspicion that clients referred to them from such 'mixed' organisations are rejects whom the consultancy/recruitment firms have not been able to place themselves.

Thirdly, to accept money from a client or an outplacement sponsor and then feed them back into another arm of your own activities runs counter to the spirit, if not the letter, of the Employment Agencies Act.